LOVE NOTES

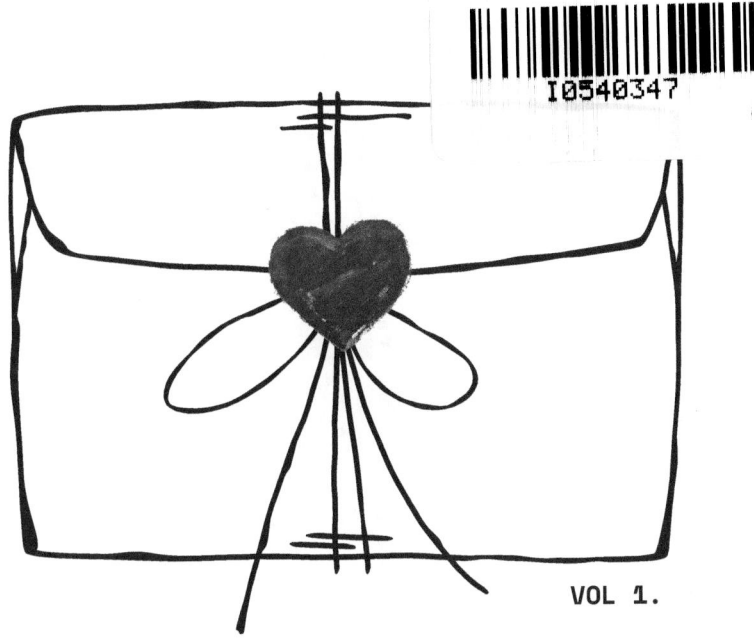

I0540347

VOL 1.

*a collection of notes,
poems & letters*

by AXEL JORDAN

LOVE NOTES

VOL 1.

to every heart that has loved, broken, and mended,
to those who have found strength in vulnerability
and courage in connection—
this is for you.

may these words remind you that love, in all its forms,
is your greatest teacher, your fiercest guide,
and your softest place to land.

with all my heart,
axel

contents

LOVE NOTES

an intimate collection of poetic, heartfelt expressions that capture the essence of love in its many forms - each note a celebration of connection, longing, gratitude, and the quiet beauty found in everyday moments shared between people.

beginnings

there's a unique magic in beginnings—the feeling of stepping into something unknown, yet utterly captivating. in the early days of love, every glance feels electric, every conversation holds promise, and the world seems to bloom in brighter colors. this chapter is a tribute to those first, unforgettable moments: the spark of connection, the thrill of discovery, and the quiet certainty that something wonderful is unfolding.

here, you'll find notes that capture the wonder of meeting someone who makes your heart race and your soul feel at home. may these words remind you of the beauty in those first steps, where every possibility feels endless and love feels brand new.

today i choose
a path that's mine
where self-belief
can truly shine
in tender steps
new seeds i sow
a love for me
where dreams can grow

in the gentle thrill
of knowing you
i feel like i'm learning
a new language
one spoken in glances
laughter and the quiet
certainty that you're the
one i've been waiting for
every moment with you feels
like the first page of a story
i never want to end
a story where each chapter
promises more joy
and more discovery
more of this beautiful
mystery that is us
here's to this beginning
to the wonder of what lies ahead
and to the feeling that with you
i've finally found home.

when i look at you
i see possibility
a world painted in colors
i've never known
a future that feels
both thrilling and safe
being with you is like standing
on the edge of
something beautiful
knowing that every step
forward brings us closer
to something extraordinary
you've awakened
a part of me that feels
alive in a way i didn't
know was possible
thank you
for this beginning
for the spark that lights
up my days
and for the promise
of all that's yet to come.

falling for you is both
beautiful and terrifying
a leap into the unknown
where my heart feels
exposed and raw and open
in ways i didn't expect
there's a quiet fear
in the possibility of loss
of wanting something
so deeply that the thought
of it slipping away
feels heavy but somehow
being with you makes
the fear worth facing
it's as if every moment
with you whispers
that love is always
worth the risk
so here i am
heart in hand
stepping into the unknown
with you
for in all this fear
there is also hope
hope that this beginning
is the start of something
real and lasting.

you're my favorite risk
the one i never saw coming
but can't imagine letting go
there's a thrill in this newness
a little fear
but mostly the feeling that
this beginning is
something worth holding onto.

your touch feels like a spark
igniting parts of me i forgot existed
with every look
every brush of your hand
there's an electricity between us
that's impossible to ignore
i feel drawn to you
like a pull i can't resist
each moment leaving me
wanting more of this
fiery beginning.

your eyes
a wild ocean's hue
pulled me in
vast and true
in their depths
i lost my way
found myself
begged to stay
a sea of calm
yet fierce and bright
a world reborn in endless light
blue horizons, secrets spun
in your gaze
i've met the one

a quiet room
the world asleep
in shadows soft
our secrets keep
a stolen glance
a held-back sigh
a brush of lips
where whispers lie
time stood still
hearts beat in code
an unmarked path
our moment showed
in hidden light, a daring bliss
the world unaware
of our secret kiss.

my first mistake
was falling for you
so sudden
so completely
i told myself
to be careful
to guard my heart
but then you came along
and all my plans unraveled
it's a risk i can't undo
a pull i can't resist
and though it scares me
i know i wouldn't take it back
sometimes the best mistakes
lead us right where
we're meant to be.

we crossed paths
like stars aligned
a fleeting glance
a spark confined
in crowded rooms
our worlds collide
a twist of fate
no place to hide
a chance encounter
brief yet bold
a story
waiting to be told
two strangers bound
by destiny's art
you walked away
but kept my heart.

shadows moving
whispers low
in hidden light
our secrets grow
eyes can't see
but senses feel
a brush of hands
a spark so real
mystery lingers
close and tight
in the velvet cloak of night
laughter soft
yet hearts beat loud
two souls lost
within a crowd
in darkness
nerves begin to fade
a quiet thrill
in secrets made
a first date
under stars unseen
where the unknown
feels serene.

sunlight dancing
warm and low
a quiet bench
where breezes flow
laughter floats
as stories spill
time stands
and all is still.
first steps taken
soft and slow
in fields
where wildflowers grow
a simple day
yet clear and true
the park the sun
and me with you.

meeting you feels
like a beautiful mistake
one that's both
thrilling and haunting
i didn't plan on this
didn't expect the way
you'd leave a mark on me
that i can't shake
it feels reckless
maybe even wrong
yet here we are
tangled in something
neither of us can ignore
if meeting you
 was a mistake
it's the one i'd make
a thousand times over.

our first kiss
was a quiet spark
a moment suspended in time
i can still feel
the warmth of it
the way everything else
simply faded away
in that one soft touch
i could sense
promises unspoken
worlds yet to be explored
it was a beginning
a breath
a heartbeat
a memory i'll carry always.

among the trees
in sunlight's glow
a boy in blue
walks soft and slow
his shirt the color
of summer skies
reflecting lakes
where freedom lies
barefoot steps
on moss and stone
the forest whispers
you're not alone
leaves dance lightly
where shadows part
nature's pulse
and his open heart
he moves like wind
calm and clear
at home in fields
with no one near
a boy in blue
in nature's grace
a gentle soul
a sacred place.

we're gunna grow old together
— 6000 miles apart

in love's first light
the world feels new
words come easy
soft and true
promises whispered
hearts laid bare
a gentle warmth
that fills the air
but early flames
can flicker fast
truths may fade
or fail to last
sweet words spoken
hopes held high
yet some are shadows
just passing by
for love at first
wears many hues
a tender truth
or half-spun muse
we learn to see
what's false what's real
as time reveals
what hearts conceal.

in the beginning
love feels like pure truth
words flow like promises
bright and sure.
yet there's a softness
a haze that can blur what's real
and what's simply wanted
it's easy to believe in forever
to trust every whispered promise
but i know
that beginnings are like dreams
beautiful yes
true—perhaps
but only time will tell
what's real beneath the glow.

where'd you go
my baby boy blue?
you were soft and gentle
but with an edge
words sharp as razors
cutting deep
each line a dagger
straight to the heart
you could throw blows
that hit harder than fists
leaving bruises unseen
where'd you go...?
my baby boy blue
who could love so fiercely
but leave such pain in his wake.

i saw you there
just a moment in the
rush and hum of the subway
you sat across from me unaware
eyes drifting over the city beyond
lost in thoughts i'll never know
there was something magnetic about you
something quiet and captivating
like you were in your own world
untouched by the chaos around us
for a split second i felt this spark
a pull wondering who you were
and where you were going
you left at the next stop
just a stranger
but a beautiful one
an echo i'll carry
even if we never cross paths again.

i didn't know it when we first met,
but something inside me just knew.
you felt familiar,
like i'd been waiting to find you all along.
now, every time i think of you,
i picture us growing old together,
side by side.
i imagine laughter in lines
around our eyes,
stories woven through our days, and a quiet
comfort that only deepens with time.
somehow, with you,
the future feels warm and certain,
like i've found the person
i want by my side, for all of it.

there's something about him
in that blue shirt,
like the color itself chose him
the shade of open skies and truth.
blue, the color of voice,
and he wears it well,
like every "i love you"
he's ever spoken comes
from a place deep and honest.
his words linger, soft and true,
like waves meeting the shore,
and i know that when he says
those three words,
he means them, steady as the sky.

your hearts
in my hand
it's beating so fast
i hope this lasts
your smiles
on my mind
where have you been
all of my life

the moment i saw you
my heart just melted
big curious eyes
a mix of innocence and wonder
trying to figure out who i was
took a few wobbly steps
then stumbled into my lap
i knew instantly—
i was yours
as much as you were mine
your tiny paws
and such soft fur
the way you nuzzled close sealed it
i fell in love
in that perfect
unforgettable moment
i didn't just get a puppy
i found a piece of my heart.

when i met my voice
it felt like meeting
a piece of myself
i didn't know was there
each note
a step into something new
a place where i could express
what words alone couldn't say
it was the beginning of a love
that would shape my soul
a journey i know
will stay with me forever.

in every sunrise
a chance to be
to start anew
to truly see
that loving myself
is where it starts
a gentle awakening
of my heart

LOVE NOTES

everyday
moments

L ove doesn't just live in grand gestures or sweeping declarations; it thrives in the quiet, familiar rhythms of daily life. this chapter honors the beauty of love in its most unassuming forms—the way it weaves into shared cups of coffee, the warmth of a hand held on a morning walk, or the laughter that fills a kitchen over a simple meal. these are the moments that, though small, build the foundation of a lasting bond.

here, you'll find notes that capture love's presence in these subtle, everyday experiences. may these words remind you of the comfort, joy, and gentle magic that come from being together, sharing life's little details, and finding happiness in the simplest of things.

in morning light
and evening rest
i find small ways
to feel my best
in every breath
a gift to keep
a love for me
that runs so deep

it's in the smallest things
your laugh
when we're cooking together
the way you reach for my
hand without thinking
the quiet moments when
we're just sitting side by side
i never realized
how much love could
be tucked into these little
everyday moments
they're simple
but they're everything
being with you
turns the ordinary
into something beautiful
and i wouldn't trade
a single second of it.

there's something so beautiful
about the way we fit
into each other's lives
even in the smallest things
the way we share
a look across the room
or how you make me laugh
at the simplest moments
it's in those little gestures
that i feel the depth of our love
i never knew the everyday
could feel so full
just because
you're by my side.

every day with you
feels like home
it's in the small things
the quiet smiles
the way we just fit
even in silence
these little moments with you
are my favorite part of life.

in stolen glances
soft and true
in simple things
i share with you
love lives here
in the quiet way
we find joy
in the everyday
no need for words
or grand displays
just you and me
in small sweet ways
a life together
gently shown
in every moment
love has grown

in whispered laughs
and morning light
in little things
that feel so right
it's here we find
our love is true
in simple moments
just me and you
no rush no need
for something more,
just everyday things
that i adore
with you beside me
all feels new
a quiet life
but bright with you

in morning light
in coffee's steam
in shared glances
quiet and unseen
love grows here
in moments small
in simple ways
that say it all
a gentle hand
a knowing smile
the way you stay
just for a while
in laughter soft
and words unspoken
these are the ties
that keep love woven
no grand display
no need for show
just everyday ways
that let us know
that here in life's
most gentle parts
we've found a home
within our hearts

in the way
your hand finds mine
or the quiet moments
that feel divine
love doesn't need
a grand display
it's in the little things
and what we say
just you and me
the world unseen
in each day's gentle
woven routine
a love that's soft
a steady beat
in everyday moments
simple and sweet

walking beside you
on this black sand beach
with the ocean stretching
endlessly before us
feels like a memory
i've always waited to live
the dark sand beneath our feet
the waves crashing in rhythm
and just us side by side
like we're the only ones in the world
there's a quiet magic here
a peace that only deepens
with each step we take together
with you even the wild feels calm
like i've found my place
right here
hand in hand.

there's something
about being here with you
high above the city of los angeles
the world feels distant
almost like it's just ours
Its wrapped in soft light
with the skyline below us
i feel a kind of peace i can't explain
as if everything we need is right here
i'll remember these nights forever
the warmth of you beside me
the city lights flickering below
and the feeling that this is exactly
where i'm meant to be.

riding bikes with you
through the english countryside
feels like something out of a dream
the fields stretch wide and green
the air crisp with that perfect quiet
just the sound of our laughter
and the wheels turning
there's a freedom here
a joy in the simplicity of it
and with you by my side
every winding path
feels like a memory we'll carry
in this moment with you
life feels wonderfully endless.

two spoons of sugar
dark and deep
a quiet love
in morning's sweep
i brew it strong
the way you crave
a small gift
in the day we pave
in every sip
a piece of me—
a gentle start
our routine's key
black coffee but sweet
just how you take
a simple act
for love's own sake

you tried so hard to resist
saying we didn't need a puppy
but the second you held her i saw it
the way your defenses crumbled
how your hands
instinctively softened around her
your bottom lip tugged down
the same way it does
when something pulls at your heart
like a boy caught
in a moment he can't resist
you were captivated
by her tiny paws and soft eyes
and i could see it clearly
she'd claimed her spot in your heart
and you weren't letting go
in that moment
it was just the two of you
and i knew
our little family had grown.

there's something so special
about cooking dinner for you
chopping stirring and tasting
each step feels like a way
to show you just how much i care
i love the way you sit nearby
maybe stealing a taste or two
sharing small laughs
and moments of warmth
when i hand you a plate
it's more than just a meal
it's my way of saying i love you
of giving a little piece of myself
hoping it brings you
the same joy you bring me.

i will cherish
every moment
i had with you.

today was one of those days
where everything felt
just a little more alive
a little more beautiful
the sun hit just right
a gentle breeze stirred the air
even the quiet moments
seemed filled with peace
it's amazing how
in the simplest parts of the day
there's so much to be grateful for
a warm cup of coffee
a few minutes of silence
the way light dances through the trees
finding joy in these small things
feels like a gift
a reminder that beauty
isn't only in big perfect moments
it's right here
in the everyday
if we just slow down enough to notice.

normally seeing appliances
all over the countertop
would drive me up the wall
but with you
i find myself smiling
every time i walk into the kitchen
each one perfectly lined up
each one you love and use near daily
somehow it's just —you
a little piece of your world
that's snuck into mine
it's funny how i've grown to love
the things i'd usually hate
all because they remind me of you
and the ways you make our home
feel full and great.

every morning
i find joy in the simple act
of making your coffee
black with two spoons of sugar
just the way you like it
there's something comforting
about the routine
the way it feels
like a quiet ritual just for us
watching you take that first sip
seeing the small smile
it brings to your face
reminds me of
all the little ways i love you
in each cup
there's a part of me
saying good morning
saying i'm here
saying i love you.

the way you make me breakfast
waking up to the sounds
and smells from the kitchen
knowing you're there
putting your care into every bite
it's you're "i love you"
but without words
the quiet thoughtfulness
that makes me feel loved
every morning you do this
and every morning
i fall for you a little more.

oh my bed
my sweetest place
soft and warm
my cozy space
a sanctuary from the day
where worries fade
a pillows touch
and dreams can play
blankets wrapped
like tender arms
pillows soft
with gentle charms
you welcome me
with restful bliss
each night a hug
each morn a kiss
when life is rough
you're always there
a quiet peace
beyond compare
my bed my love
my truest friend
in your embrace
no worries the end

good morning
enjoy your coffee and smile
cause you are so very loved.
— favorite morning notes

with my arms
wrapped around you
through the mountains of thailand
feels like pure freedom
the wind rushes past
and the world blurs
but i can feel
every beat of my heart
steady against your back
it's just us
the winding roads
and the endless sky
and in this moment
nothing else matters
i feel alive and fearless
and completely in love
holding onto you
as we carve our own path
through these wild
beautiful hills.

i never thought i'd say this
but the way you chew
that loud crunch
makes me smile every time
normally that sound
would drive me crazy
but with you it's different
somehow it's become
one of those little things
that i look forward to
something endearing
and uniquely you
it's like a sweet reminder
that even the smallest quirks
make me love you more.

lets spend our mornings
remembering
to take moments
to love ourselves
then lets spend
the rest of the time
loving each other.

cooking for you
is one of my favorite ways
to show you how much
you mean to me
there's something special
in every part of it
choosing the ingredients
adding the herbs and spices just so
making sure everything
is cooked to perfection
i love the delicate details
dressing the plate beautifully
setting the table and pouring your drink
it's like a quiet ritual
a way of wrapping my care
my affection and love all into one
knowing you'll sit down and enjoy it
makes every moment in the kitchen
feel worthwhile
it's my way of saying
i see you
i love you
i want you to feel
taken care of.

in the quiet moments
when my fingers graze
the piano keys
i find peace
playing even a simple melody
fills my day
with something richer
a reminder that music
lives in the small things too
it's these everyday moments with music
that make everything
feel more alive
more meaningful.

in small routines
i find my grace
a daily rhythm
a gentle pace
self-care blooms
in moments small
a quiet love
that lifts it all

LOVE NOTES

longing & distance

love, when stretched across distance, takes on a new depth, where every missed touch and unspoken word lingers in the heart. longing transforms love, making it both tender and bittersweet, filled with memories cherished and reunions imagined. this chapter is a tribute to those who feel the ache of love across miles, time, or circumstance—the ones who wait, who hold onto hope, and who find ways to keep love alive even when apart. here, you'll find notes that echo the resilience and beauty of love that endures separation. may these words remind you that love, though distant, is no less powerful, and that true connection transcends even the greatest divides.

where'd you go
my baby boy blue?
once soft and gentle
warm and true
but now your words
like razors slice
a dagger's aim
no thought of price
your hands once soft
now fists that throw
hard blows that strike
both fierce and low
a fire burns
where calm once grew
where'd you go
my baby boy blue?
a love turned sharp
a gentle heart gone
lost somewhere
no light of dawn
the boy i knew
fades from view,
where'd you go
my baby boy blue?

though space may stretch
and time may part
i keep myself
within my heart
in distance
i stand strong and free
a steady love
i hold for me

being away from you
is harder than i ever imagined
i miss the simple things
the comfort of having you close
the way we'd talk about our day
or just the warmth of you next to me
distance makes every day
feel a little heavier
every goodbye lingers a little longer
but even though it's hard
i know that what we have is worth it
loving you from afar isn't easy
but it's a reminder
of how deeply i feel for you
and i'll hold onto that
even across the seas.

there's something so sweet
about the way
you fall asleep
pillow to screen
like it's our own way
of closing the distance
makes it feel a little easier
a little closer
i love that you
just want us to end
the night together
as if we're sharing
the same space
with only a screen
in between.

thirty thousand
feet above
sky-bound
driven by our love
counting down the hours and miles
each one closer to your smile
pressed against this tiny space
dreaming of your warm embrace
a journey through the clouds and blue
all roads and skies
lead me to you

miles blur beneath a rolling sky
with each step closer
my heart beats high
a journey made
not just to roam
but to bring you back
to bring you home
your hand in mine
as paths unwind
leaving distant cities behind
the world feels right
no longer alone
together now
our hearts in our home

fighting is hard enough
but being so far apart
makes it feel even worse
i hate that
i can't just hold you
look into your eyes
and feel the comfort
of being near
it's like the miles between us
make every word sharper
every silence heavier
i know we'll work through this
but i wish i could reach
across the distance
close the gap
and let you know that
despite everything
my heart is still right here with you.

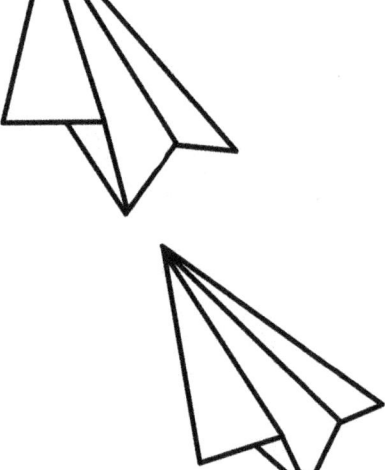

and so i sit...
perched over my phone
awaiting your name
to appear on the screen
and so i sit ...
thousand of miles apart
from the one i wish
to hold in my arms
and so i sit ...
dreaming of ways
to bring us
together from apart
may your heart
be lit from the fabric
thats keepings
up apart.

there's an ache
i didn't know existed
a hollow feeling
i can't quite put into words
trust is such a fragile thing
something we built together
piece by piece
and now
it feels shattered and scattered
i don't know where we go from here
but i know things have changed
i wish it were different
that this part of our story
didn't have to hurt so deeply
somehow i'm left
somewhere between love and loss
wondering if we can ever
find our way back.

being away from you
is harder than i thought it'd be
i miss the little things
the closeness we had
distance makes it tough
but it also shows
me how real this is
because no matter how far
my heart is still with you.

it's hard to wrap
my head around the hurt
the trust that's been broken
i thought that we
we were stronger than this
built on something real
now i'm left
questioning everything
wondering if what we had
can ever be whole again.

i crossed a line
i can't erase
shadows are left
in our sacred space
a moment's lapse
a reckless fall
now echoes haunt
each silent call
i see the hurt
within your eyes
the trust i broke
the love that dies
if i could turn
and start anew
i'd mend the heart
that once felt true
mistakes like mine
they leave a scar
a distance deep
so close yet far
i know i lost
what mattered most
now left to hold
this hollow ghost

i trusted you
heart open wide
built dreams with you
stood by your side
but in the shadows
lies were spun
a love thought ours
a love undone
your words once warm
now cut and fray
promises made
now swept away
i search for reasons
but none will fit
just echoes now
where truth once lit
a broken vow
a line you crossed
the weight of love
the cost a loss.
i loved you deep
i loved you true
but now i'm left
to heal from you

you turned away
crossed unseen lines
your promises left
in scattered signs
a trust once whole
now torn apart
i'm left to mend
this broken heart

i miss you in ways i can't fully explain
it's the quiet moments
the empty spaces
where you should be
the small things i want to share
with you but can't
life feels a dimmer without you here
like i'm waiting
for everything to feel right again
until then
know that you're in every thought
and every heartbeat
i'm counting down the moments
until i'm with you again.

this isn't easy to say
and it hurts to write
but i think we both know
things have changed
i care about you deeply
and part of me will always
hold onto the memories we've made
but somewhere along the way
we've grown apart
and i feel that we're no longer
the best for each other
i hope you find happiness
and i hope you know
that you'll always hold
a special place in my heart
i'll never forget
what we shared.

i miss you
i love you
but i've decided
i'll never tell you again
some things
are better left unsaid
even if they're still true.

you cheated
with our friend
behind my back it was
now you expect to hang out
but sex was all it ever was

i've thought about this
and i just don't
see a future for us anymore
things haven't been working
and i need to move on
i hope you can understand
but it's time to let this go.
— it ended with a text

wearing your hoodie feels
like wrapping myself in you
like a quiet hug
when you're not here
it smells like you
soft and familiar
and somehow
it makes me feel safe
and close to you
even when we're apart
it's just a hoodie
but with it i carry a piece
of you through my day
like you're right here with me.

your kiss
your glance
your smile
your touch
it's like you never left
your taste lingers
and i want more
my blue eyes beauty
i can't read your thoughts
i can't read past those eyes
in my dreams
i see them
teary eyed
looking up at me.

my feelings haven't faded
but i've made my peace
with keeping them to myself
as some things
are better left unspoken
and even though
theres part of me
that aches for you
i know it's time to let it go
so i'll hold
these words quietly now
and in silence
they'll stay with me.
— words unshared but forever true.

there's something
irresistible about you
the way your intensity
draws me in
its the warmth in your eyes
and that undeniable passion
a fire i can't ignore
every glance leaves me
wanting more
being close to you is electric
like a spark
i can't shake.

close your eyes
count to three
you're here with me
it'll be like nothing
no now don't you cry
it'll be just fine
to say goodbye
we were down to nothing
and though we wasted away
our love will stay
just not today
at least we can say
we still had something.

when you find this
we may be 1000's
of miles apart
just know you're
always in my heart
stay being you
don't every change
for anyone
i love you.

i am right beside you
whenever you need me.

you deserve the world
— note found in my luggage

when i sing
i feel a connection
that spans distance and time
reaching places i can't touch in person
music is my bridge
my way of reaching
loved ones far away
of filling the space between us
with each note
i close the distance
feeling as though somehow
we're not so far apart after all.

even when far
i hold my own
in the space between
i've know i've grown
self-worth anchors me
through the ache
a love for me
no distance can break

thank you
for all you do
even though
you're far away
you have made me
a better person
— note after first separation

LOVE NOTES

gratitude & appreciation

● n love, gratitude brings depth and warmth, turning
1 ordinary moments into cherished memories. this
chapter is a celebration of the thankfulness that blooms
when we take a step back and truly see our partner—their
kindness, their laughter, their unwavering support.
appreciation transforms love into something even more
meaningful, reminding us of the gift it is to love and be
loved in return.

here, you'll find notes that express the heartfelt gratitude
that makes love richer and more profound. may these
words inspire you to savor every moment, to acknowledge
the little things, and to treasure the unique bond you share.

for every friend
and gentle hand
for love that helps
me understand
i'm grateful in
the simplest ways
a quiet thanks
that fills my days

in each small joy
i lift my gaze
for gratitude
has endless ways
a whispered thanks
a soft refrain
for love and life
through joy and pain

thankful for each flaw
and for each grace
i meet myself
with warm embrace
in self-respect
and quiet pride
a love for me
no need to hide

for morning light
and evening stars
for every scar
that made me ours
i bow in thanks
a gift to hold
for love that's warm
for life that's bold

at one time
i though all men
were like my dad
harmful
violent
neglectful
cheaters ... you changed my mind

i overheard you talking
about the way we used to be
you said you were
the lucky one
but the lucky one
was me.

you changed me
you made me strong
you made me wise
you made me tough
you made me rough
you made me smile
you saved my life
— note to self

saw you across the room
and i couldn't believe my eyes
a light so beautiful
that i knew right away
i wanted you to be mine
and now
with how I move
its me and you

the way you see me
actually see me
is more
than i could
have ever imagined.

gratitude blooms in quiet ways
in whispered thanks
and softer days
a gentle warmth
a steady light
that fills our hearts
so soft yet bright
it's found in moments
small but true
in morning sun
in skies of blue
in kindness shared
in love's embrace
in life's sweet words
the endless grace
gratitude hums in every part
a quiet joy that fills the heart
for all we have
for all we've known
it's gratitude
that leads us home

you had no idea
how much i needed that
your simple hello
on a day where
everything went so wrong did
when i felt invisible and lost
you sat down beside me with a smile
you didn't know the weight i was carrying
the loneliness that wrapped around me
but you showed up anyway
asking how i was
giving warmth without a second thought
that small kindness meant more
than you'll ever know
in that moment
you reminded me of
the goodness in the world
and that simple act of care saved me
thank you for being the light
i didn't know i needed.

gratitude whispers
soft and clear
a thankfulness
that draws us near
in small delights
and moments spare
we find a peace
beyond compare
each day a gift
each breath a grace
gratitude's light
in every place

being compassionate
is about more than kind thoughts
it's about the way we show up to listen
and offer understanding
when we practice compassionate presence
we focus on being fully engaged and attentive
both with ourselves and others
without judgment or the need to fix things.

i'm grateful every day
for the gift of music
it has given me purpose
helped me through
my darkest times
and brought light
when i needed it most
i thank the piano
my voice and every song i've sung
and every melody i've played
for bringing me closer
to myself and giving me a way
to share that with the world.

compassionate presence
allows us to hold space
for our own emotions
and those of others
it's about understanding
that being there and truly listening
can sometimes be
the most healing act of all
whether it's sitting with a friend in silence
allowing yourself to feel without
needing to change anything
or holding space for yourself
in moments of challenges
compassionate presence
creates an atmosphere
of acceptance and trust.

sitting there on lovers deck
thinking back to when we met
we couldn't tell
when or where sun set
even when it felt so right
too scared to hold on tight
distracted by the love
we left behind
but you—
it was always you
and i'm on my way
back to you.

i appreciate
all that i have
and all that i am becoming
— note to self

i don't say it enough
but i'm so grateful for you
for all the little things you do
without even thinking
your kindness
your patience
the way you're there
in ways that feel
so steady and sure
i'm thankful for every laugh
every quiet moment
and every time you've listened
when i needed it most
you're my safe place
my teammate and my friend
and knowing i get to share
this life with you fills me
with so much gratitude
thank you for being
exactly who you are.

i am grateful
for the strength
and resilience of my body
— note to self

having you as my partner
is like having someone
who truly sees me
 you don't just listen
you hear me
and that's something
so rare and beautiful
when i share my thoughts
my needs and my worries
you take them to heart
and show me that they matter
knowing you're willing
to make changes
to grow with me
makes me feel valued
in ways i can't fully explain
it's a gift to be with someone
who cares so deeply
who doesn't just say they love me
but shows it in every way
i feel seen and heard
and truly loved with you.

i am grateful
for the beauty
and joy in my life
— note to self

i thank myself
for the strength i bear
for every step
for each soft care
self-acceptance
fills my core
a gratitude i can't ignore

i just love
how much i love you.

to the ivory keys
you've been more than just an instrument
you've been a lifeline
a place where my thoughts
my emotions and dreams come to life
each key holds a piece of my story
a way to express
what words could never capture
you've taught me patience and discipline
and the beauty of getting lost
in something greater than myself
through you i've found a voice
i didn't know i had
a space where i can feel and create without fear
you've transformed my life
note by note
song by song
thank you for being
the constant i return to
for letting me find myself
 in your melodies
my heart will always belong
to the music you bring to life.

LOVE NOTES

enduring love

L ove that stands the test of time becomes a quiet, steadfast presence—a steady rhythm that beats through every season of life. enduring love is found in the commitment to grow together, to weather life's storms, and to rediscover each other anew, again and again. this chapter celebrates the strength of a love that deepens over time, grounded in trust, patience, and the beauty of shared history.

here, you'll find notes that honor love's resilience and the gentle power that comes from staying beside one another, year after year. may these words remind you of the beauty in love that lasts, a testament to the journey you share and the bond that only grows stronger.

through every storm
i stay the course
a love for me
my steady force
unshaken faith
in highs and lows
self worth that only
deeper grows

and all along
you are beauty
right where you are
you were there
right from the start
since back when we
were young
i don't know
where the time has gone
we've been in love
for so long
since back when we
were young

our love has been through so much—
time and distance
ups and downs
and yet here we are
stronger than ever
enduring love isn't always easy
it's built with patience and forgiveness
and choosing each other over and over again
i'm grateful every day
for the depth we've grown into
or the way you stand by me
and for the quiet strength we share
loving you isn't just a feeling
it's a choice i make each day
knowing that whatever comes
we'll face it together.

in 30 years
we'll be married for 30 years
and i can't wait
to see the wrinkles of love
on our faces
created by laughter and love
created by memories
compassion & forgiveness
starting now
from this moment i say "i do"

through every season
and every storm
we're still here
enduring love
is quiet and steady
something i hold
close every day
loving you
is my constant
my anchor
and i wouldn't
trade it for anything.

forgiving you
hasn't been easy
it's been a process
facing the hurt
letting go of the anger
and slowly piecing back together
the trust that was broken
but deep down i know
that love
isn't always about perfection
it's about growth
understanding
and finding a way forward
even through the pain
i'm choosing to forgive
to let this be a part of our story
that makes us stronger
i hope we both learn from this
and maybe just maybe
we'll come out of it closer than before.

love is quiet
love is loud
a gentle warmth
or thundercloud
it's in the touch
the whispered word
in silent moments
deeply heard
a spark a fire
a steady beat
love makes us whole
makes life complete

you can smile if you want to
close your eyes if you want to
take your time because i want you
hideaway if you want truth.

forgiveness is hard
but i'm willing to try
i can't erase the pain
but i believe in second chances
in learning and rebuilding
let's see if we
can make this work
one step at a time.

every time
i try to walk away
you start a fight
so i would stay
every time
you make me change my mind
and now i'm found
every little
move you make
we break up
but we won't break
you're everything
i want to be around
now i'm found.

hey sugar
why you look so sad
take my hand
we'll skip a beat
i'll make you laugh
hey sugar
life ain't what it seems
take a breath
count to ten
and come lay with me
sweet darling
lay down your head
close your eyes
unclench your fist
we'll make it
as long as we try
keep going
it's worth the ride
remember the days
remember the nights
when i made you smile
when i drove you wild
on wilton place.
—rdm → fd

i'm here
waiting for your name
to light up my screen
waiting to hear your voice
i can almost hear it already
that soft, sleepy "good morning"
with your eyes barely open
there's something so sweet
in that sound
makes everything feel softer
i wait for it like a little ritual
like a quiet promise
that today
will be a good day because
you started it with me
just your voice
it's such a simple thing
but it's everything.

we're in a rough patch right now
but even through the hard days
i feel the strength of our love
i know we're both
feeling the weight
and it's not always easy
but i also know
we're strong enough
to make it through
i believe in us
in the way
we hold each other up
when things get tough
and in the love
we've built together
it's worth every effort
every difficult moment
because i know
that on the other side of this
we'll be even stronger
our love can endure this
i'm certain of it.

my sweet man
i appreciate
you venting last night
and speaking your mind
i heard you
and hope to be a better partner
to you in the future
the long term goal
is growing together
— early moments notes

our love
isn't just about the good times
it's woven into every challenge
we've faced together
through all the highs and lows
there's a steady
unbreakable thread
that holds us together
enduring love
isn't flashy or loud
it's quiet and constant
like a heartbeat
it's the love that stays
a love that forgives
and it grows stronger
with every test
i'm grateful every day
for the love we share
for the way we choose each other
no matter what comes our way
this kind of love is rare
and i wouldn't trade it for anything.

being loved
is like finding
a place to rest
where you don't have to pretend
or try too hard
it's the feeling of warmth
in the simplest moments
a hand reaching for yours
a voice that says "i'm here"
when the world feels too big
it's knowing someone
sees all of you
even the parts you try to hide
and still chooses to stay
being loved
is like coming home to yourself
feeling safe and understood
and deeply valued
it's a quiet kind of magic
that makes everything
feel a little brighter
a little more real.

there's something about
this sweater that feels like home
it's soft and warm
and carries the faintest hint of you
your scent and your presence
the comfort only you can give
when i slip it on
it's like wrapping myself
in an embrace from miles away
a piece of you that stays with me
it's my favorite sweater
not just because it's cozy
but because it reminds me of you
of every moment
we've shared in it
i feel safe and held
and somehow closer to you
it's not just a sweater
it's you.

getting through
hard times isn't easy
it takes more than just
hoping for better days
it's about showing up every day
even when it feels
like nothing's changing
even when the weight
feels too heavy
it's in those tough moments
that staying persistent
and consistent matters most
each step and each effort
brings you closer to the light
even if it feels small
remember
every challenge faced
builds resilience
every tough day
you overcome
strengthens you
keep going
you're stronger
than you think
and this too will pass.

through trials faced
and storms survived
i see my worth
undimmed and revived
a love for me
enduring and whole
the steady keeper
of my soul

dear older me,
i know you carry a lot of weight and sometimes
you blame yourself for the tough times i went
through. but i want you to know—it's not your
fault. none of it is. i don't see you as someone
who failed me; i see you as someone who got me
through it all. i look at you and see strength, the
kind i can only dream of having. i want to be as
strong as you, as big and tall and brave as you
are.
you're everything i look up to, my best friend, my
hero. thank you for being there, for protecting me,
for keeping me safe when i felt scared or small.
even on the hard days, you never gave up, and I
admire that more than you know. i'm grateful for
every way you've taken care of me, for every
choice you made to make sure i could grow up
safe.
i love you. i hope you can see yourself the way I
do, strong and caring, a protector through it all. I
wouldn't be who i am without you, and i wouldn't
want anyone else by my side. thank you for being
you.
forever,
— lil you

148

music is my lifelong companion
a love that has endured
through everything
it's been there for me
when i was at my highest
and held me together
when i was at my lowest
this love for music
has only deepened over time
steady and true like a heartbeat
that keeps me moving forward.

dear lil me,
i'm so sorry that it's been so tough for you. i wish I
could have been there sooner, to protect you from the
hurt, to keep you safe from all the pain you felt. i know
there were times you felt alone, unloved, even broken.
I know you felt unwanted, and i'm sorry you had to
carry that weight. but i want you to know, all that
sadness and emptiness you feel right now—it won't
last. i promise you, there's so much love waiting for
you. soon, you'll feel surrounded by people who truly
care about you, who see you for who you are and love
you deeply. you'll smile every day, and it won't feel so
hard anymore. you're going to be strong, so strong
that you'll barely recognize the fear or the loneliness
you feel now. you're never alone, even when it feels
that way. I'm here with you, always. in every tough
moment, every time you feel you can't go on, know
that i'm here beside you, cheering you on, guiding you
forward. I know it's tough right now, but keep going.
trust me, you'll be so glad you did. you are loved,
more than you realize. and soon, you'll feel it every day.
with all my heart,
— big you

LOVE NOTES

self - love

a t the heart of every relationship lies the foundation of self-love—the ability to embrace oneself fully, with kindness, compassion, and understanding. this chapter is a gentle reminder that love begins within, that nurturing our own hearts allows us to give and receive love more openly. self-love is an invitation to honor our own journey, to recognize our worth, and to fill our lives with a love that doesn't rely on anyone else.

here, you'll find notes that celebrate the beauty of loving oneself. may these words encourage you to find strength, joy, and peace in your own company, and to cherish the person you are becoming each day.

the day begins with the soft light of morning filtering through the window, a gentle reminder that this is your time. you start by making a cup of coffee, its warmth filling your hands and sparking the first moment of calm. you savor each sip, feeling the energy settle in, readying you for a day of care and purpose.

for breakfast, you treat yourself to something nourishing, something that feels like a gift to your body—a meal that speaks of freshness and intention, prepared with love and attention. it's a small act, but in this, you're already honoring yourself.

as the morning stretches on, you carve out time for creativity. you open your new book, letting yourself get lost in its pages, your mind expanding and inspired. then, you find your way to your own words, whether it's writing a few lines, capturing thoughts that have been circling, or allowing yourself to explore whatever stirs within you. you're creating not just for others, but for the joy it brings you.

in the afternoon, you cook an incredible meal just for you.
you take your time, savoring the act of chopping,
seasoning, tasting—a reminder of the artistry and care in
even the smallest details. you plate it beautifully, and as you
sit to eat, there's pride in what you've created, a small
celebration of you.
the day winds down with moments dedicated to quiet,
reflecting on the strides you've taken toward happiness, on
the pride you feel in yourself, on the fullness of your heart
and soul. you end the evening feeling balanced, whole,
grateful for the time you've given yourself to grow, to
create, and to care.

in mirrors clear
i see the truth
a beauty felt
since early youth
in self kindness
i find my ground
a love for me
that's safe and sound

i searched for love in endless places
in distant dreams and strangers' faces
but somewhere deep a voice began
a quiet truth "love who i am"
in every scar in every flaw
a strength emerged the beauty raw
no need for more no need to roam
self love became my steady home
a love that's mine
both fierce and true
a light that shines from me to you
for in myself i've found the key—
the love i need lives here in me.

change can feel unsettling
and it often brings self-doubt
during times of transition
self compassion can be the gentle
anchor that helps us find
peace amidst uncertainty
when we approach change with kindness
we give ourselves permission to be human
to make mistakes
and to grow at our own pace
self compassion during change
means allowing ourselves
the space to adjust
to be imperfect
and to learn without harsh criticism
it is a reminder
that we deserve kindness
especially when navigating new
or challenging paths
by practicing self compassion
in times of change,
we can find stability within ourselves
creating a sense of safety
and resilience
that carries us forward.

i am free from the
weight of the past
— note to self

how does it feel
when love comes
how do you bleed
when it goes
isn't it hard
to see it die
but some kinds of love
must say goodbye.

to you, who is capable of tremendous greatness,
i know things feel heavy right now, like the weight of
everything is pressing down, making it hard to see beyond
this moment. but remember, these tough times are just
part of the journey—every challenge, every tear, is guiding
you somewhere beautiful, even if you can't see it yet.
allow yourself to be guided. let yourself feel every emotion,
without judgment. cry when you need to—those tears are
part of the healing, a release for the soul. laugh when you
can, even if it feels small or fleeting. let joy sneak in where it
may, because it's those moments, however brief, that
remind you of the light within. know that every dark tunnel
leads somewhere brighter. you may not know exactly
what's at the end, but it's there, waiting for you. keep going,
step by step, knowing that self love is not about being
perfect but about accepting yourself through everything.
you're resilient, you're capable, and you are worthy of all the
light and joy that life has to offer.
with love,
— the you, living our greatness

you are so much more
than what you see

i am enough
just as i am.
— note to self

i'm a beautiful work
in progress
sometimes
i'm on top of the world
and sometimes
i'm rolling down a hill
but i'm always growing.

i am worthy
of love
and respect.
— note to self

i love
and honor
who i am becoming.
— note to self

"becoming"

you are not who you were
yet not quite who you'll be
in the in-between you rise
unfolding steadily
through the cracks, you reach
in each fall you find grace
for growth is a journey
not a single hurried race

breathing in
i calm my body
breathing out
i smile

i am my own
both soft and strong
a place to rest
where i belong
in flaws and grace
i see my worth
a love that blooms
from me
for me first

i am strong
i am resilient
and i am capable
of handling anything
that comes my way.
— note to self

"kind thought"

with each kind thought
i rise anew
i am enough
and i am true
in self-compassion
i find my way
a love that holds
me every day

i am grateful
for this moment of life.
— note to self

when i sing
or play the piano
i feel myself more whole
music is my reminder
that i am enough just as i am
it's in those moments
lost in a song or a melody
that i feel truly connected to myself
free from doubt or judgment
music has taught me to love
and accept myself in ways
i never thought possible.

loving yourself isn't selfish
it's the foundation of everything
we can build together
when you love yourself
you'll be freer to love me without fear
without holding back
without questioning
what you deserve
you'll shine in ways
you don't even realize you can
and that's the person
i want to share my life with
the person who knows
how remarkable they truly are.

i attract prosperity
and success
in all areas of my life.
— note to self

i am worthy of healthy
loving relationships.
— note to self

i am constantly
growing and evolving.
— note to self

i am calm
relaxed and at ease.
— note to self

my dearest self,
there is something incredibly powerful about loving
yourself exactly as you are. it's an act of bravery, a quiet but
bold declaration that you are worthy of your own love. self
love is a journey, not a destination—it takes time, patience,
and a gentle heart.
when you look at yourself, remember that you are not just
the sum of your flaws. you are your dreams, your kindness,
your resilience, and so much more. take moments to honor
the incredible person you are becoming. stand up for
yourself, prioritize your needs, and let go of the urge to be
perfect.
loving yourself doesn't mean you're done growing; it means
you embrace each step with compassion. know that you are
enough, and that you deserve the same love and respect
that you so freely give to others.
with love,
— your biggest fan

i am gentle
and patient with myself
as i heal.
— note to self

my love,
i need you to know how much you mean to me, how
deeply i care for every part of who you are. but there's
something i see in you that i hope you can see too—a
version of yourself that's tender toward the pieces you
sometimes hide away. i love you, all of you, but i need
you to love yourself too.
you give so much of yourself to me, to us, and it's
beautiful. but the truth is, to be the partner i know you
want to be, you have to start with you. i want to see
you nurture yourself with the same care and devotion
you show me. i want to see you believe in your worth,
not because i do, but because you feel it in your own
soul.
so please, my love, take the time to care for
yourself. learn to embrace your flaws, your fears, your
beauty, and your strength. know that i'm here to
support you every step of the way, but this journey has
to start within you. for us to thrive, you need to thrive
too.
with all my heart,
— axel

i am surrounded by love
light and positivity.
— note to self

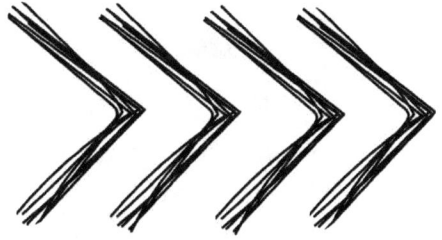

LOVE NOTES

legacy of love

ove leaves an indelible mark, creating connections that
transcend time and space. this chapter is dedicated to
the love that lives on—a legacy passed from one
generation to the next, the quiet strength in friendships,
and the lasting bonds with family and loved ones. this is the
love that shapes us, comforts us, and remains with us long
after the people we cherish are gone.
here, you'll find notes that honor the enduring impact of
love across lifetimes and relationships. may these words
remind you of the timeless gift that love offers, a legacy that
touches lives, lingers in memory, and lives on in the hearts
of those we leave behind.

the love i give
lives on in you
a quiet strength
a bond so true
in each embrace
a story told
a legacy
that's mine to hold

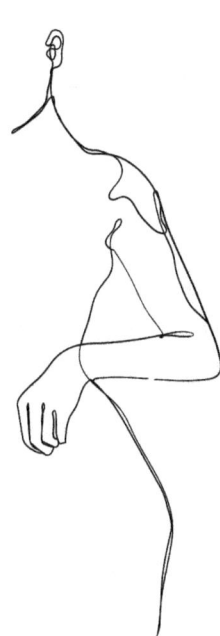

through every lesson
and every care
my love will find you
always there
a gift passed down
both soft and strong
a lasting love
that lives so long

in gentle acts
and hands held tight
i pass along
my heart's own light
for a love
that's simple
and deep and pure
is the type of love
that will endure

in every bond
i choose to keep
a love that runs
both strong and deep
i pass it down
a gentle guide
its something that
i hold with pride

the care i give
the love i share
is shaped by ways
i've learned to care
in self-worth
grown from roots of grace
a hug is more
than each embrace

through every hand
i've held in grace
my love lives on
in time and space
a part of me
in all i give
a part of me
that learns to live

the greatest gift i can leave you
isn't wealth or possessions
it's the love that's guided me
shaped me and brought me here
i hope that in my actions
in my words
and in my care
you see the foundation
of something lasting
i may not have all the answers
but i want you to know
that love is at the heart of it all
take this knowledge
and carry it forward
knowing that wherever life takes you
you'll always have
this love to ground you.

baby girl danni
you're cute and uncanny
your mood is anything but mellow
you make me happy
like j-e-l-l-ooo
— love as written by a 7-year old, East London

i've carried the weight
of your absence
your actions
and the pain they left behind
for so long i thought forgiveness
meant letting go of what i felt
but now i understand
it's about freeing myself
i forgive you
not because what happened was okay
but because i need to let go
of the anger and hurt
i see now
that you carried your own struggles
battles i'll never fully know
i release this burden
and in doing so i find peace
i wish you healing
and i'm choosing
to move forward
with love and compassion.

the warmth i give
the care i show
are seeds of love
i watch grow
in each kind act
a gift i leave
a legacy in
which i believe

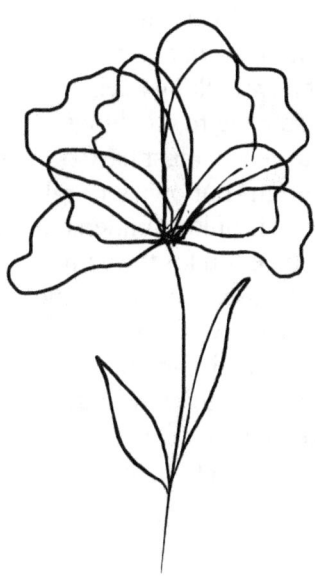

growing up
you made things hard for me
the bruises
the names and the broken things
they left scars
not just on my skin
but in my heart
i felt alone and small
and for a long time
i held onto that hurt
but now looking back
i'm starting to see things differently
i realize you must have been going
through your own struggles
things i couldn't understand back then
i forgive you for the pain
for the way you pushed me away
i hope you've found peace
just as i'm finding mine
i'm letting go of the past
and i hope we can move forward
both of us a little lighter.

grandma:
why don't you want
to come over anymore?

me:
because you love
thiago more
and i'm just left alone

grandma:
my love
i don't love
your brother more
he just needs more love
and attention than you do

— one of the last conversations with my grandmother
before she passed. i began to see myself more clearly after
this.

friendship can be
more profound than family
it's the bond we choose
not the one we're born into
friends are the ones who see us at
our most vulnerable
and love us because of it
they're the ones who know our quirks
and our fears
they know our laughter
they're there in our first joys
and our first heartbreaks
showing us who we are
and what we're capable of
friends become our first mirror
reflecting back the person we're growing into
and sometimes the one we don't want to be
but friendship isn't always easy
it can hurt deeply too
sometimes friends drift or disappoint us
revealing sides we hadn't expected
yet it's the highs and lows
the strength and imperfections
that make friendships so rich and lasting
they shape us in ways nothing else can
friendships teach us about trust
and resilience and ultimately
about the beauty and messiness
of connection.

with you i always knew
there was more
beneath the surface
a quiet unspoken love
felt in every small gesture
and in every embrace
its in the way
your hand would linger
when it brushed mine
there was always
that something extra
that 'could-have-been
i felt your affection
and i sensed your wish
for it to be more
but something held us both back
maybe it was a fear of losing
the closeness we had
or simply a respect for the line
we never crossed
thats the beauty of true friendship
to be so close that it feels
like a kind of love beyond romance
a bond that's deep and intimate
without needing to be anything else
you've given me a kind of affection
that has been constant and true
and while we never took that other path
i'll always cherish the closeness we shared
a friendship like ours built on trust and love
and the understanding is its own kind of forever.

every day
i come to the cemetery to visit you
i know it sounds silly
to talk to the ground
but it brings me a kind of peace
you were the only person
i could really open up to
and now even though you're gone
sharing my thoughts with you
feels like a connection i can't let go of
being here
talking to you
makes me feel like you're still listening
still right here with me
i miss you more than words can say
i wonder sometimes
what it'll be like when i leave
when I can't come here every day
to be near you
a part of me stays here with you
no matter where life takes me
but for now i'll keep coming
because this is something i still need
a way to hold onto you
and feel close even if just for a
little while.

dear dad,
i forgive you—for your absence, for the hurt, for leaving,
and for all the times you weren't there when i needed you
most. i forgive you for forsaking me, for the space you left
behind. i've come to realize that my ultimate father was the
guidance i received from my angels, those unseen hands
that held me and lifted me up when you couldn't. they gave
me the strength and love i was missing.
looking back, i see now that i was never truly alone—just
without you, and while that absence shaped me, it didn't
break me. i've found peace in knowing i was watched over,
cared for in ways you couldn't provide. i'm letting go of the
pain and embracing the life i've built with that guidance.
may you find your own peace, wherever you are.
with forgiveness,
— me

working the entrance gates at hollywood forever cemetery, i grew accustomed to familiar faces among the visitors, each carrying their quiet reverence or grief. but one boy stood out. he was young, maybe twelve or thirteen, and every day, he came to sit by a new plot—unmarked but filled. at first, i thought little of it. many found solace in silence, and he seemed no different. but as the days passed, i noticed the intensity in his face. he'd lay beside the plot, his grief almost tangible, heavy and raw. yet there was something else—a calm anticipation, as if he were visiting a friend. each day, he arrived with sorrow but left with a soft smile, as though comforted.

months went by, and i couldn't help but wonder about his visits. one afternoon, i finally asked. he told me he came to see his grandmother, the only person he felt he could talk to. her passing had left him lost, and this was where he could still speak to her about everything. his grief made sense then, and i understood the peace he found there. one day, though, his smile was gone. he walked out, carrying a weight that seemed too much to bear. after that, he never returned. i often wonder what happened to him— if he found his peace or simply said goodbye for the last time. but i'll always remember him, the quiet boy who brought his heart to the cemetery and left each day with a little less of his grief.

— entrance gates, hollywood forever cemetery, *2023*

music connects us to our roots
to the stories and songs
of those who came before us
each note carries a memory
a reminder that we're part
of something greater
something timeless
my love for music
is part of that legacy
one that i hope to carry forward
sharing its beauty
with those who will come after me.

music is woven into
the very fabric of who we are
it's more than sound
it's a feeling that vibrates
through every cell
its an energy that fills us
moves us and reminds us that we're alive
we feel it deep in our bones
that rhythm that pulses and connects
as if every beat speaks a language
our hearts already know
each note— each chord
it feels like a memory
a piece of our own story
bringing us back to moments
we thought we'd forgotten
or emotions we didn't know
we needed to feel
in a way
we're made of music
created from the signatures
of rhythm and harmony
it's in the way we walk
the way we laugh
even the way we breathe—our own
unique melody playing quietly within
to love music is to love something eternal
something that connects us all
in ways we can't always explain
but always understand.

dear mom,

you taught me so much. my capacity to forgive comes from watching you, from the lessons you showed me, even when life was at its hardest. but along with that, i learned a lack of boundaries from you too. i watched as the men in your life belittled you, hurt you, and tried to diminish your worth, and i saw how you stayed—whether out of fear of being alone or out of need. i watched life harden you, piece by piece.

but i also watched a light in you that never faded. no matter what, you lit up a room with your presence, your beauty, your spirit. people were drawn to you, loved being near you, felt lifted just by your energy. you were hurting, but that brightness in you never completely dimmed. i see that strength, that resilience, and i love that part of you deeply. i'm thankful for the heart you passed down to me, and for the lessons, even the hard ones.

i only wish i understood what happened in your life that made you love yourself less. because to me, you were always enough. you deserved to feel that too. i hope, somehow, youknow how loved you truly are.*

with all my love,

— me

i honor myself
in what i give
in lessons learned
and love i live
my self worth echoes
deep and wide
a legacy
i hold with pride.

ms, king

i don't know if you'll ever see this, but i wanted to finally say thank you. you changed my life, and i never really got the chance to tell you. you were the first person who showed me what my voice could do, how to express myself in a way that felt freeing. i still remember standing in that doorway, listening to the choir - i was in kindergarten, feeling so small yet somehow seen, and it was all because of you. you welcomed me into music that day with open arms, taught me to sing, to feel, to let my voice carry the things i didn't have words for back then.

you protected me and guided me when i needed it most. those early days with you set me on a path i couldn't have imagined, and i carry the things you taught me every day. i've wondered many times what happened to you, where you are now, and i hope you know how much of an impact you made on me. your kindness and encouragement left a mark on my life that i still feel today.

so, thank you, ms. king. thank you for your patience, your guidance, and for seeing something in me, even when I couldn't see it myself. I wouldn't be who i am without you. with all my gratitude,

— j.j.g.

LOVE NOTES

true feelings

t rue feelings are the foundation of any lasting connection—the raw, unfiltered emotions that lie beneath the surface. they aren't always easy to express, but they're the heartbeat of a relationship, the essence of what makes love real. this chapter is a celebration of vulnerability, the courage it takes to share your deepest thoughts, fears, and desires with someone you trust. here, you'll find notes that reveal the soul's truest sentiments—the words spoken in moments of honesty and intimacy. may these pages remind you of the beauty in being seen and accepted for who you are, and the power of sharing your heart without holding back.

in every truth
my heart lays bare
a love for me
that meets me there
no mask to hide
no shield to hold,
just honest words
both brave and bold

when feelings rise
unguarded and real
i find the strength
to let them heal
for in each truth
a freedom grows
a deeper love
a path that shows

in moments when
i can't pretend
i let my heart break
then let it mend
a love for truth
so raw and bright
a guiding flame
a steady light

in honest words
and quiet ways
i find the strength
to meet my gaze
a love for all
i truly feel
in each confession
soft and real

every thought
laid bare to see
a gentle trust
i hold in me
true feelings flow
both soft and strong
a melody grows
that's all my own

in rawest thoughts
and honest cries
i find the strength
to not disguise
a gentle love
for all i am
in every truth
my heart i span

latin men
you have a way about you—
confident and such passion
and that magnetic energy
you can feel across a room
its something
that's both bold and warm
like a spark waiting to ignite
every time i'm with you
i feel that heat
that pull
and i can't help
but be drawn in
wanting more.

i remember
how it was
i remember
the things i use to say
i remember
the thought of it
before i walked away
no more thinking
about the days
with my heart full
i walked away
no more trying
to find the ways
or thinking
of words to say

just when i thought it would end
my ex would walk back in
use to say they were okay
use to make it all go away
but the ex was still a problem
my ex would ignore the call
too busy on their fall
my ex would escape in the pipe
the smoke like fruit
for him—just right

the word "addiction" carries a heavy weight—for those who openly acknowledge their struggle and for those who silently suffer without admitting. as someone who faces my own addiction head-on, in therapy and through daily effort, i don't think it's fair to be labeled as the one "struggling." i work hard every day to overcome it, yet i see others freely feed their addictions without a second thought, believing that's just how life is. empathy should extend to all of us, but there's a difference between fighting to grow and choosing to stay unchanged. sympathy, however ... have sympathy towards yourself instead of on me.

sometimes
i still think of my ex
but not in the way one would think
i left and never looked back
and i know that hurt him
i hope he became
a better version of himself
because i sure did.

to you, whom i haven't forgotten,
it's hard to put into words the ache i feel. with you, i felt
everything all at once—love, happiness, sadness, anger,
frustration, pain, confusion, pleasure, and hope. being with
you was like riding a wave that could lift me higher than i'd
ever been and crash me deeper than i knew was possible. i
loved you deeply, and every part of me wanted us to work,
to find a way through.
i asked you, time and time again, to change. i could see
what was coming; i knew, somehow, that one day, i would
hit my limit. i knew that the moment i had enough, i'd walk
away and never look back. it's as if i could see the future the
moment i'd become numb, unable to feel any more of the
highs or lows. and i knew that's when you'd change, that
only then you'd realize what you'd lost. but by then, it was
too late. i was already gone, my heart closed off from the
feelings that once burned so fiercely. i wanted to stay, to
keep fighting for us, but there's only so much a heart can
take. so i left, carrying the memories of everything we
shared but no longer able to feel their weight.
i walked away from you and all that we were, knowing it
was the only way to find peace.
i hope one day you understand. this wasn't how i wanted
our story to end, but maybe this was the only way it ever
could have.
with all the feelings i no longer hold,
- he, who walked away

there's no easy way to say this, but i feel like my heart has changed. i care about you deeply, and you've been such an important part of my life, but the love i once felt isn't there in the same way. i've tried to hold on, to feel that spark again, but somewhere along the way, things shifted. it's not about something you did or didn't do—it's just that my feelings have grown distant, in a way i didn't expect and can't seem to bring back.

i want you to know that this isn't easy for me to say, and it doesn't change how much i value you or the memories we've made. you deserve love that feels as true and whole as it once did between us. i'll always care about you, but i know we both deserve more than what i can give right now. this is hard, but i feel it's the most honest way forward.

— when its finally time to leave

the passion of my latino
the desire in his eyes
the fire in his thighs
the cleverness of his lies

to you, who had the strength to walk away,
i read your letter and felt every word sink in, knowing each
one was true. i can't deny the rollercoaster i put you
through, the mix of highs and lows, and the way i held back
when i should've changed. i thought you'd always be there,
that somehow we'd keep holding on through everything,
despite my own actions pushing you away. i know now
how unfair that was—to keep you hoping, asking, waiting
for a change that came too late.
i felt it too, the love and the chaos, the way we burned so
brightly together. i thought if i provided you with enough,
it would be enough. i see now that providing alone wasn't
what you needed; you needed me to meet you in your hurt,
to make things better instead of just letting them build. i
didn't realize that every moment i held back was a moment
that chipped away at what we had, leaving you with less
and less to hold onto. i can't blame you for leaving. i wish
i'd seen it all clearly before we got here, before you reached
that point of numbness, before you became a stranger
walking away. before i could never contact you again ...
before i never heard from you again. if i could go back, i
would do things differently—i'd hold you close without
waiting until i'd lost you. i'd listen, really listen, to the
things you needed me to change, and i'd put in the effort to
make it right. all i can do now is say that i'm sorry. for every
hurt, every time i pushed you aside, every moment i held
back when you needed more. i'll carry the lessons you left
me with, and i only wish i'd learned them sooner. i hope
that wherever you are, you find peace and happiness,
because if anyone deserves it, it's you.
take care,
- he, who sits with the regret of losing you

in my truest self
i find release
the love of me
a quiet peace
each feeling honored
every part
a gentle holding
of my heart

oh golden crunch
a flavor so fine
with each bite
i know you're mine
a love affair in every taste
you linger
leaving no crumb to waste
dusty fingers
hands aglow
bright as sunshine's early show
with every nibble
my heart ignites
a snack like you
is pure delight
a guilty pleasure
a cheesy dream
a beloved treat
in every scene
my heart it knows
no other foes
than you my dearest ... cheetos

music gives me a voice
to express my truest self
even when words fail
when i sing
or play the piano
i feel raw and open
unafraid to share
the parts of me
that remain hidden in silence
each note
each chord
is a piece
of my heart laid bare
music lets me speak
from a place of honesty
a place where i can feel deeply
and be fully seen.

in letting go
of fear and pride
i find my truth
no need to hide
for love begins
when walls come down
in honest words
where trust is found

each feeling
raw and true
a glimpse of me
i share with you
for in this space
i stand so real
in every word
my heart i feel

true feelings
speak in silent ways
in open nights
and softer days
a love for me
that lets me be
in every truth
completely free.

LOVE NOTES

heartache

h eartache is the shadow side of love, a testament to the depth of what once was. this chapter is dedicated to the moments when love is lost, strained, or broken— when pain and longing replace the warmth we once knew. heartache isn't just sorrow; it's a reminder that love, even when it hurts, is powerful and transformative. here, you'll find notes that speak to the ache of letting go, the silence after goodbye, and the journey toward healing. may these words offer comfort, understanding, and a reminder that even in pain, there is a path forward. heartache shapes us, but it doesn't define us; it's a chapter, not the whole story.

in echoes of
what used to be
i find the courage
to set me free
a love for self
both scarred and true
in heartache
i am born anew

through tear streaked nights
and silent cries
i find my strength
as sorrow dies
in every ache
a whispered grace
a love for me
takes heart's embrace

in hurt's embrace
i find my way
through darkest night
to light of day
for heartache though
it burns and tears
leaves room to heal
and breathe fresh air

you called me to watch the sunset
and pointed the camera forward
so i could see your view
it was a beautiful sunset
but not on camera
were four bike wheels
and not just two
not on camera
were two hands intertwined
not on camera
was a shared kiss
it was a beautiful sunset.

why is it
that when it ends
we remember
all the happy moments?
why is it
we hold onto the laughs?
why don't we see the pain—
why do we lose sight
of how we got here?

where is the night
you came to me
and told me
all you wanted to be?
remember the things
we would say
when days just slipped away?
i found out who you are
but now you're with somebody new
how could this be—
he's not me
it's a love tragedy
here i am
i made my plea
i'd go down on broken knee
i promised you
i'd break your fall
it's our love tragedy

why did we fight
was it the lies?
we were so blind
we couldn't see
don't mean to intrude
but step away and you'll see
i'll find love eventually
you try to run
you try to hide
to keep your feelings inside
saying that you deserve the best
my best is better than the rest.

in your eyes
i remember
what it felt like
to say goodbye
even in our
hardest moment
i still loved you.

"24 hours"

it's been 24 hours
since i last heard from you
i used to think it was me
or that i was the problem
i later understood
you used us as an excuse
to feed your habit
it was your disguise
in those 24 hours
you became someone else entirely
a person i still never knew
in those 24 hours
you lost every bit of me
and i lost every bit of you.

pain feels worse
when its caused
by those you love most
i used to hide from it
or pretend it didn't bother me
i never wanted
to feel like a victim
but eventually
it caught up to me
i realize now
i fell into it
taken advantage of
pain feels worse
when its caused by
someone you love.

heartache lingers
heavy and deep
in quiet nights
where shadows creep
echoes of laughter
now a ghost
the memories of
what we cherished most

a touch that fades
a look that's gone
the silent ache
of moving on
yet in this pain
a strength is found
a way to stand
on hollow ground
heartache molds
it bends and breaks
and from the shards
new life awakes
for even in
the darkest part
love leaves a mark
it shapes the heart

i chose you over him
because my heart
has been broken too many times
each time i hoped he'd change
that things would be different
but hope
only carried me so far
you came into my life
like a reminder
of what love is supposed to be
steady and kind
and without
the sharp edges that cut deep
it wasn't easy to walk away
but i knew i had to choose
the love that nurtured me
and not the one that hurt
with you
i feel a healing of heart
and that's a feeling
i won't let go of.

you were my best friend
the one i trusted
with everything
but you betrayed me
and that cut deeper
than words can say
i held on for far too long
hoping you'd change
that you'd care enough
to fix what you broke
but trust once shattered
doesn't come back.

in pain's deep ache
i still remain
a love for me
through joy and strain
self-care—a balm
both soft and true
a way to heal
to start anew

i've made peace
with letting go
i've stopped waiting
for apologies
that will never come
and i hope one day
you understand
what you lost
this is goodbye.

mom,
for a long time, i believed that i wasn't good enough. i
carried the thought that you gave me up because i wasn't
perfect, that somehow i wasn't deserving of love. those
insecurities haunted me, weaving their way into so many
moments of my life and making me question my worth over
and over.for a long time, i believed that i wasn't good
enough. i carried the thought that you gave me up because
i wasn't perfect, that somehow i wasn't deserving of love.
those insecurities haunted me, weaving their way into so
many moments of my life and making me question my
worth over and over.
but as i grew, so did my understanding. i began to see that
your decision must have been incredibly difficult, that
letting me go was a choice made out of love, not rejection.
it wasn't about me not being enough; it was about
circumstances that i'll never fully know. that realization
didn't come easily, but it brought me a sense of peace.
with time, i learned to forgive you. it took years to let go of
the feelings of being unwanted and to recognize that we're
all just human, making choices with what we know at the
time. i forgive you for the pain, for the unanswered
questions, and for the space that your absence created.
i want you to know that i've found my way. i am loved, i am
whole, and i know now that i am enough. wherever you
are, i hope you've found peace too. you will always be a part
of me, and for that, i carry a piece of love for you in my
heart.
holding space for continued peace,
- the child you gave away

losing a dog
feels like losing a part of your heart
it's not just the absence of a pet
it's the silence that fills the house
where once there were
the soft thuds of paws
and the gentle jingling of a collar
it's the emptiness in the routine
the moments when you reach out
instinctively to touch their fur
only to be met with nothing but air
the loss seeps into everything
the quiet mornings
that used to start with a wagging tail
the evenings
where their warmth would rest against you
and the simple joyful moments
that made life better.

note to my lil men,
grief for a dog is complicated because it's not just sadness;
it's the memory of unconditional love. dogs love with a
purity that's hard to find anywhere else. they are
companions who never judge, who seem to know when
you need them most, and who stay by your side with a
loyalty that's unwavering. losing that kind of bond feels like
losing a piece of your soul, the part that knew only love and
light when they were around.
to you, sweet boy riley, mr. poots tatum, and old man jinx,
you were all so loved and so very missed. there's a unique
loneliness that comes with it, a space in your life and heart
that stays empty. it's in the way the house feels a little
colder, quieter. the absence of their presence makes you
realize just how much they were a part of your family, your
daily life, and even your sense of self.
yet, amid the sorrow, there's a whisper of gratitude—a
thankfulness for having had that kind of love at all. it's a
pain that is as deep as the joy was bright. the memory of
their playful eyes, the sound of their bark, and the feel of
their head resting on your lap remain, not just as a
reminder of loss, but as a testament to the love that was
real and will always be cherished.

to you
who lived on 45th street
you shattered me that night
you hurt my body
broke my heart
and scarred my soul
what you did changed me
left me altered in ways
i couldn't undo
the touch of another
hasn't felt the same since
you remain nameless
but your face
is one i will never forget.

to my sweet lil girl,
know that i wanted more than anything in this world. but
wanting you and being able to give you what you needed
were two different things. my life was a mess. i was fighting
demons and drowning in addictions, and i knew deep
down that i'd only mess you up if you stayed with me. you
deserved more than me,, more than the chaos i was living
in. you deserved love, safety, and a real chance at happiness.
you were my hope, the light that kept me going in the
darkest moments. carrying you was the only time i
managed to stay sober for longer than i thought i could. i
felt a purpose i'd never known before. i was determined to
not make you like me. but as much as i loved you, i couldn't
shake the truth that my love alone wasn't enough to beat
the demons inside me. the only way i could really love you
was to let you go, even if it broke me. i remember holding
you, looking at your tiny hands and face, and feeling a love
so deep it hurt. you were so beautiful, so perfect. i called
you "hope" in my heart because that's what you were to me.
walking away, knowing i'd never hold you again, felt like a
part of me was being ripped apart. but i did it because i
wanted you to have a life that wasn't touched by my
struggles. i don't know who you are now or where life has
taken you, but i pray every day that you're safe and happy. i
hope you grew up feeling loved and cared for. my sweet
hope, i need you to know that even though i wasn't there,
you were loved. it wasn't perfect. it was full of flaws and
pain, but it was real and it was the best i had to give.
wherever you are, i hope you know your worth, and i hope
you're surrounded by love. you were the best thing i ever
did, my greatest hope, and you'll always be in my heart."
- bellevue hospital, 1996

heartache whispers
in the night
a fading flame
a lost light
but through the dark
a pulse remains
a quiet hope
beneath the pain

"thorns"

thorns have a way
of reminding you
that beauty can hurt
even after they poke
and draw blood
there's something
about the rose
that calls you back
it's as if the pain makes
the sweetness of the scent
even more precious
a reminder that
even the most beautiful things
come with their risks
you reach for it again
knowing the thorns are there
but hoping this time
the touch will be gentler
that the beauty
will be worth it
and somehow
even with the sting
it always is.

watching your memory fade away
feels like growing out
of a movie you once adored as a child
you cling to the anticipation
waiting for the moments
that once made your heart race
you play them in your mind
hoping to feel that same thrill
but when they come
the spark is gone
the magic has faded
and you realize that time has moved on
the period has passed
leaving only echoes of what once was.

tonight i tried
to make your favorite meal
we've been over for a while now
and i haven't been able
to bring myself to cook it since
but i love it
and i missed it
so i decided to try
i burned it
now i'm sitting here wondering
if i did it on purpose
or by accident
maybe it was my way
of holding on to the memory
or maybe it was a reminder
that some things
are meant to stay in the past.

heartache
is a quiet persistent ache
that lingers
even in the best of times
it's the emptiness
where someone used to be
the moments when memories
flood back with a bittersweet sting
heartache is learning to carry
a love that no longer has a place to go
it's the sharp reminder
of what once was
and the slow heavy process of letting go
but within it
there's a strange kind of beauty
a reminder of how deeply we can feel
how much we're capable of loving
and maybe in time
that ache will soften
leaving only the memory
of love that once was.

"toxic partner"

a toxic partner may weaponize the most intimate parts of your life, using your vulnerabilities, experiences, or personality against you in moments of conflict. this betrayal is hard to reconcile, as it leaves you doubting not just the relationship but your value and judgment. what makes it even more difficult is that these behaviors don't always disappear when the relationship ends. they leave a lasting impact, triggering thoughts of inadequacy and self-blame. you may find yourself stuck in the cycle of trying to "fix" things, hoping the good moments will return. but when the pain outweighs the joy, and your self-worth begins to erode, it's time to face the truth: the relationship has reached its end.

even when you know a relationship is toxic, breaking free can feel impossible. this is not just an emotional struggle but a chemical one. love triggers the release of powerful hormones like dopamine, oxytocin, and serotonin — chemicals that make you feel connected and euphoric. when mixed with toxic patterns, these hormones create a cycle of addiction, pulling you back toward the relationship even when it causes harm.

i walked around for hours
just to avoid going home
the place we once shared
now feels destroyed and empty
far from the safe haven
it used to be
how did we get here?
was your pain really that deep?
was mine so unaware?
now all that's left
are questions without answers
and the understanding
that there's no going back.

being cheated on
feels like a betrayal
in the deepest sense
it's a wound that reaches
down to your core
a trust shattered in ways
you didn't think were possible
it makes you question everything
your worth your choices
even the moments
you thought were real
there's an emptiness
a confusion as if you've lost
a part of yourself
that you can't quite get back
it's a hurt that doesn't just fade
it lingers
challenging you to rebuild
from the inside out
but through it all
it's also a painful reminder
of your strength and resilience
because while it breaks you
somehow piece by piece
you begin to heal.

when i'm lost
in heartache
music is my shelter
it's the language
of sorrow and comfort
a place to release
what feels too heavy
to hold alone
my piano keys carry my pain
turning it into something beautiful
something that can be felt but not lost in
through every melody
i find healing
a way to mend
even the deepest cracks
in my heart.

through wounds
and scars
i come to see
the worth and strength
inside of me
self-care heals
where shadows grow
a tender love
i've come to know.

coming soon

LOVE NOTES
volumes
2 & 3

a final note

as this journey comes to an end, i hope these pages have felt like a soft place to land—a safe space to feel, to reflect, and to remember. love is a complex and wondrous thing—it grows, it changes, it challenges, and it heals. it has the power to lift us higher than we ever imagined and to ground us in the quietest, most personal moments.

whether love has brought you joy, taught you resilience, or left you with questions, it's been a part of what shaped you. in each note, i hope you've found a piece of yourself. i hope you've felt seen, understood, and reminded of the profound power of connection—whether with another, with yourself, or with the memories that linger. these pages are an ode to love in all its raw, messy, and beautiful forms.

if there's one truth to leave you with, it's this: hold onto love in all its forms. let it soften you, let it guide you, and let it remind you of who you are. even in its hardest moments, love has the power to carry you forward, to reshape you, and to bring you home to yourself. wherever your journey leads next, know that love will always be your truest companion.

with love,
axel

Other works by Axel Jordan

SONS & SHADOWS
HEALING (of) HEARTS
365 Days Of Affirmations

coming soon,

The Journey Back
Beyond Lust

about the author

Axel Jordan is a celebrated author, visionary musician, master certified sound healer, and certified CBT & REBT coach practitioner with an innate ability to transform emotion into art. A storyteller at heart, Axel's work is rooted in his personal journey—a life shaped by love, loss, resilience, and self-discovery. Through his writing, sound therapy, and coaching, Axel creates spaces where others can explore the depth of their emotions and connect with the beauty of their own humanity.

Born and raised in Brooklyn, NYC, Axel's vibrant cultural upbringing and passion for creative expression have profoundly shaped his perspective on life and love. In *LOVE NOTES*, Axel presents a tender and deeply personal collection of notes, poems, and reflections on love in all its forms—its joy, its heartache, its transformative power. Each page invites readers to explore the complexity of love, to find solace in shared experiences, and to embrace the beauty of connection.

Known for his ability to guide others through healing with compassion and authenticity, Axel's work spans the realms of music, wellness, and emotional growth. His sound healing practice, infused with celestial alchemy, and his coaching expertise reflect his commitment to helping others find peace and strength within themselves.

When he's not writing or curating transformative sound healing experiences, Axel cherishes quiet moments with his partner and their foster animals, embodying the love and tenderness that echo through his work. *LOVE NOTES* is an extension of his life's mission: to honor the power of love, connection, and self-expression, and to remind readers that love—above all else—is worth holding onto.

www.AxelJordanBooks.com

Cover Design: Axel Jordan

ISBN: 979-8-89686-148-5

Library of Congress Control Number: 2024926372

ATTENTION: SCHOOL AND BUSINESSES

Any published works of Axel Jordan are available at quantity discounts with bulk purchase for educational, business, or sales promotional use.

For information, please contact:
www.AxelJordanBooks.com